Table of Contents

Introduction

Part I: Understanding Client/Customer Relationships

Part II: Nurturing Client/Customer Relationships

Part III: Leveraging Technology and Automation

Part IV: Scaling Through Client/Customer Relationships

Conclusion

- The Power of Client/Customer Relationships in Business Growth
- Looking Ahead: Continuing Your Entrepreneurial Journey

Introduction

Welcome to the Entrepreneurial Journey

Congratulations on embarking on the exhilarating and rewarding journey of entrepreneurship! Whether you're a seasoned business owner or a budding entrepreneur, you're about to embark on a thrilling adventure filled with challenges, triumphs, and endless opportunities for growth.

As you set out on this entrepreneurial voyage, it's essential to recognize that success in business isn't just about having a great idea or offering a groundbreaking product or service. It's about understanding the intricate dynamics of client/customer relationships and leveraging them to drive sustainable growth and success.

The Importance of Client/Customer Relationships

At the heart of every successful business lies its relationships with its clients and customers. These connections form the bedrock upon which businesses are built, fueling growth, driving innovation, and fostering loyalty and advocacy.

In this introductory section, we'll delve into the critical role that client/customer relationships play in the entrepreneurial journey. From understanding the fundamentals of these relationships to harnessing the power of technology and automation, we'll explore the strategies and techniques that will empower you to cultivate strong, lasting connections with your clientele and propel your business to new heights of success.

Join us as we embark on a journey to unlock the secrets of effective client/customer relationship management and discover how these relationships can serve as the cornerstone of your entrepreneurial endeavors. Together, we'll explore the strategies, tools, and best practices that will empower you to build meaningful connections, drive growth, and achieve your entrepreneurial dreams.

Part I: Understanding Client/Customer Relationships

Welcome to Part I of our journey towards mastering client/customer relationships. In this section, we delve into the fundamental aspects of understanding and nurturing these critical connections that form the backbone of any successful business venture. By grasping the intricacies of client/customer relationships, you'll be equipped with the knowledge and insights necessary to forge lasting bonds, drive growth, and foster a loyal customer base.

Defining Client/Customer Relationships

At the core of every business lies its relationships with clients and customers. In this section, we'll explore the essence of these relationships, defining what it means to truly connect with those who support and drive your business forward.

The Psychology of Client/Customer Interactions

Understanding the psychology behind client/customer interactions is essential for effectively engaging with your audience. From the principles of human behavior to the dynamics of emotional intelligence, we'll uncover the keys to fostering meaningful connections and building rapport with your clientele.

Building Trust and Credibility

Trust forms the foundation of any successful relationship. In this segment, we'll delve into the strategies and techniques for building trust and credibility with your clients/customers, earning their confidence and loyalty through transparency, integrity, and reliability.

Effective Communication Strategies

Communication is the lifeblood of client/customer relationships. Here, we'll explore the art of effective communication, from active listening to clear and concise messaging. Learn how to convey your brand's value proposition, address concerns, and foster open dialogue to strengthen connections with your audience.

Understanding Customer Needs and Preferences

To truly serve your clients/customers, you must first understand their needs, desires, and preferences. In this section, we'll delve into the importance of customer empathy and market research, uncovering insights that drive product innovation, personalized experiences, and customer-centric solutions.

Join us as we embark on a journey to master the art of client/customer relationships. Through a deeper understanding of these foundational principles, you'll gain the tools and strategies needed to cultivate loyal, engaged customers who champion your brand and contribute to its long-term success.

Chapter 1
Defining Client/Customer Relationships

In the bustling world of entrepreneurship, success often hinges on the strength of relationships—specifically, the relationships forged with clients or customers. But what exactly do we mean by client/customer relationships?

At its core, a client/customer relationship embodies the dynamic interplay between a business and those it serves. It's not merely a transactional exchange of goods or services for money; rather, it's a multifaceted connection built on trust, mutual understanding, and value creation.

Consider this: when a customer walks into your store, clicks on your website, or engages with your brand in any way, they're not just seeking a product or service. They're seeking an experience—an experience that resonates with their needs, desires, and aspirations.

Client/customer relationships encompass various dimensions:

Transactional Aspect: This involves the exchange of goods, services, or information for monetary compensation. It's the foundational element of any business interaction, but it's only the tip of the iceberg.

Emotional Connection: Beyond the transactional aspect lies the emotional bond between the business and its clientele. This bond is nurtured through personalized interactions, empathetic understanding, and genuine care for the customer's well-being.

Trust and Reliability: Trust is the bedrock of any lasting relationship. Clients/customers rely on businesses to deliver on their promises consistently, whether it's in the form of high-quality products, dependable services, or transparent communication.

Long-Term Value: Successful client/customer relationships extend beyond a single purchase or transaction. They are about fostering loyalty and creating enduring value for both parties over time.

Feedback Loop: Effective relationships are characterized by open channels of communication. Clients/customers should feel empowered to provide feedback, share their experiences, and voice their concerns, allowing businesses to adapt and improve continuously.

Now, you might wonder: why are these relationships so crucial for small business owners?

The answer lies in their transformative potential. Strong client/customer relationships can drive business growth, fuel word-of-mouth referrals, inspire brand advocacy, and ultimately, differentiate your business in a crowded marketplace.

As we journey through this book, we'll explore strategies for cultivating and nurturing these relationships, delving into the psychology of client/customer interactions, building trust and credibility, mastering communication techniques, and aligning your business offerings with the evolving needs and preferences of your clientele.

But before we dive into those strategies, it's essential to grasp the fundamental essence of client/customer relationships—the bedrock upon which your entrepreneurial success rests.

Chapter 2
The Psychology of Client/Customer Interactions

In the intricate dance of business, understanding the psychology behind client/customer interactions is akin to mastering the choreography. Every move, every gesture, every word carries weight, shaping the perception of your brand and influencing the decisions of your clientele.

To navigate this dance effectively, let's explore some key psychological principles at play:

First Impressions Matter: The adage "you never get a second chance to make a first impression" rings especially true in business. Studies show that people form lasting judgments within milliseconds of encountering a new person or entity. Whether it's your website, storefront, or initial interaction, strive to make a positive and memorable impression.

The Power of Reciprocity: Humans are wired to reciprocate kindness and generosity. By offering value upfront—whether through informative content, personalized recommendations, or exceptional service—you can trigger a sense of indebtedness in your clients/customers, fostering goodwill and loyalty in return.

Social Proof and Influence: We often look to others for cues on how to behave or what choices to make. Leveraging social proof—such as customer testimonials, reviews, or endorsements—can bolster your credibility and influence the decisions of prospective clients/customers.

Emotional Engagement: Emotions play a pivotal role in decision-making. Businesses that can evoke positive emotions—such as joy, excitement, or trust—in their clients/customers are more likely to forge lasting connections and inspire loyalty. Whether through storytelling, empathetic communication, or experiential marketing, aim to create emotionally resonant experiences.

The Principle of Scarcity: People tend to place greater value on things that are perceived as rare or exclusive. By strategically employing scarcity—such as limited-time offers, exclusive deals, or product scarcity—you can stimulate urgency and drive conversions.

Cognitive Biases: Human cognition is riddled with biases—mental shortcuts that influence our perception and decision-making. From the anchoring effect to confirmation bias, understanding these biases can help you craft more persuasive messaging, optimize pricing strategies, and design compelling offers.

The Importance of Trust: Trust is the cornerstone of any successful relationship, including those between businesses and their clientele. Establishing trust requires consistency, transparency, and reliability. By fulfilling promises, addressing concerns promptly, and maintaining ethical standards, you can cultivate a sense of trustworthiness that underpins long-term relationships.

As a small business owner, recognizing and leveraging these psychological principles can empower you to orchestrate more impactful and meaningful interactions with your clients/customers. By understanding the drivers behind human behavior, you can tailor your approach, refine your messaging, and ultimately, deepen your connections with those you serve.

Chapter 3
Building Trust and Credibility

In the dynamic landscape of business, trust is the currency upon which relationships are built, and credibility is the beacon that guides clients/customers to your doorstep. Whether you're a seasoned entrepreneur or a budding startup, establishing trust and credibility is paramount for sustainable success.

So, how can you cultivate these essential qualities within your business? Let's explore some strategies:

Consistency is Key: Consistency breeds familiarity and reliability. Whether it's delivering consistent quality, adhering to deadlines, or maintaining brand messaging across channels, strive for reliability in every interaction with your clients/customers. Consistent experiences build trust over time.

Transparency and Authenticity: Transparency builds trust by fostering open and honest communication. Be transparent about your business practices, pricing structures, and product/service offerings. Authenticity—being true to your values and genuine in your interactions—resonates with clients/customers on a deeper level, fostering trust and loyalty.

Deliver Exceptional Value: Going above and beyond expectations demonstrates your commitment to your clients/customers' success and satisfaction. Whether it's providing exceptional customer service, offering personalized recommendations, or creating added value through bonuses or perks, strive to exceed expectations at every turn.

Establish Authority and Expertise: Positioning yourself as an authority in your industry builds credibility and instills confidence in your clients/customers. Share your knowledge through educational content, thought leadership articles, or speaking engagements. By showcasing your expertise, you reinforce trust in your capabilities and offerings.

Social Proof and Testimonials: Testimonials, reviews, and case studies serve as powerful social proof of your credibility and the value you deliver. Encourage satisfied clients/customers to share their experiences publicly, whether through written testimonials, video testimonials, or online reviews. Positive feedback from others validates your business's reputation and encourages trust among prospective clients/customers.

Build Relationships, Not Transactions: Shift your focus from short-term transactions to long-term relationships. Invest time and effort in building genuine connections with your clients/customers, understanding their needs, and providing personalized solutions. By prioritizing relationships over transactions, you foster trust and loyalty that transcends individual interactions.

Handle Mistakes Gracefully: Mistakes are inevitable, but how you handle them can make all the difference in building trust. Own up to errors, apologize sincerely, and take swift action to rectify the situation. Demonstrating accountability and a commitment to making things right reinforces trust in your integrity and reliability.

Stay True to Your Promises: Your word is your bond. Consistently delivering on your promises—whether it's meeting deadlines, honoring guarantees, or fulfilling commitments—builds trust and credibility over time. Be mindful of what you promise and ensure you have the resources and capabilities to deliver.

By incorporating these strategies into your business practices, you can lay a solid foundation of trust and credibility that fosters enduring relationships with your clients/customers. Remember, trust is earned through consistent actions, transparent communication, and a genuine commitment to delivering value. As you build trust and credibility within your business, you pave the way for long-term success and growth.

Chapter 4
Effective Communication Strategies

Communication serves as the lifeblood of any successful client/customer relationship. It's the conduit through which ideas are exchanged, needs are understood, and connections are forged. As a small business owner, mastering effective communication strategies is essential for building rapport, resolving conflicts, and fostering trust with your clientele. Here are some key strategies to consider:

Active Listening: Effective communication begins with listening. Practice active listening by giving your full attention to your clients/customers, seeking to understand their perspective, and acknowledging their concerns or feedback. Repeat back what you've heard to ensure clarity and demonstrate empathy.

Clear and Concise Messaging: In a world inundated with information, clarity is paramount. Ensure your messages are clear, concise, and easy to understand. Avoid jargon or technical language that may confuse your audience. Tailor your communication to resonate with your clients/customers' needs and preferences.

Adaptability: Every client/customer is unique, with their own communication style and preferences. Be adaptable in your approach, adjusting your communication style to match the needs and preferences of each individual. Whether it's through email, phone calls, video conferencing, or face-to-face meetings, tailor your communication to suit the situation and the preferences of your audience.

Empathetic Communication: Empathy is the cornerstone of effective communication. Put yourself in your clients/customers' shoes, seeking to understand their feelings, concerns, and motivations. Communicate with empathy and compassion, demonstrating that you genuinely care about their well-being and success.

Transparency and Honesty: Trust is built on a foundation of transparency and honesty. Be forthright in your communication, providing accurate information and avoiding misleading statements. If you encounter challenges or setbacks, communicate openly and honestly with your clients/customers, and work together to find solutions.

Timely and Responsive: In today's fast-paced world, timeliness is crucial. Respond promptly to inquiries, messages, and requests from your clients/customers. Even if you don't have an immediate answer, acknowledge their communication and provide a timeframe for follow-up. Timely responsiveness demonstrates your commitment to customer service and fosters trust and reliability.

Use of Visuals and Multimedia: Visuals can enhance the effectiveness of your communication by conveying information more quickly and engagingly than text alone. Incorporate visual elements such as infographics, charts, and videos to illustrate key points, simplify complex concepts, and make your messages more memorable.

Feedback Mechanisms: Establish clear channels for feedback and communication with your clients/customers. Encourage them to share their thoughts, suggestions, and concerns openly, and demonstrate that you value their input. Actively solicit feedback through surveys, polls, or one-on-one conversations, and use it to inform your decision-making and improve your services.

By implementing these effective communication strategies, you can strengthen your relationships with your clients/customers, foster trust and loyalty, and differentiate your business in a competitive marketplace. Remember, effective communication is not just about conveying information—it's about building connections, understanding needs, and nurturing meaningful relationships that drive long-term success.

Chapter 5
Understanding Customer Needs and Preferences

To thrive in today's business landscape, it's crucial to move beyond a transactional mindset and delve deep into the psyche of your clients/customers. Understanding their needs, preferences, and pain points lays the groundwork for meaningful interactions, tailored solutions, and long-lasting relationships. Here's how you can gain a comprehensive understanding of your customers:

Conduct Market Research: Start by conducting thorough market research to gain insights into your target audience. Identify demographic information such as age, gender, location, income level, and occupation. Understand their psychographic traits, including attitudes, values, interests, and lifestyle choices. Utilize surveys, focus groups, interviews, and data analysis to gather valuable information about your customers' preferences, behaviors, and purchasing habits.

Listen and Observe: Actively listen to your customers' feedback and observe their actions to uncover hidden insights. Pay attention to their verbal cues, nonverbal signals, and purchasing patterns. Engage in conversations with your customers to understand their motivations, challenges, and aspirations. Use this qualitative data to refine your products, services, and marketing strategies to better align with their needs and preferences.

Create Buyer Personas: Develop detailed buyer personas that represent your ideal customers. These fictional characters embody the characteristics, goals, pain points, and preferences of different segments of your target audience. Use demographic and psychographic data to flesh out your buyer personas, including their job roles, daily routines, media consumption habits, and communication preferences. By personifying your customers, you can tailor your marketing messages, product offerings, and customer experiences to resonate with their unique needs and preferences.

Utilize Data Analytics: Leverage data analytics tools and techniques to gain actionable insights from your customer data. Analyze quantitative data such as website traffic, conversion rates, customer interactions, and sales metrics to identify trends, patterns, and opportunities. Use predictive analytics to anticipate future customer behaviors and preferences, enabling you to proactively meet their needs and deliver personalized experiences.

Stay Agile and Responsive: The needs and preferences of your customers are constantly evolving in response to market dynamics, technological advancements, and societal trends. Stay agile and responsive to these changes by continuously monitoring customer feedback, market trends, and competitive developments. Embrace a culture of experimentation and innovation, iterating on your products, services, and marketing strategies based on real-time insights and customer feedback.

Provide Value-Based Solutions: Align your offerings with the needs and preferences of your customers by focusing on value-based solutions. Understand the specific problems, challenges, and goals that your customers are trying to solve or achieve. Position your products and services as solutions to these pain points, emphasizing the tangible benefits and outcomes that they deliver. By addressing customer needs and providing value-driven solutions, you can differentiate your brand, build customer loyalty, and drive business growth.

By prioritizing a deep understanding of your customers' needs and preferences, you can build stronger connections, drive customer satisfaction, and foster long-term loyalty. Remember that successful businesses are customer-centric, continuously striving to anticipate and exceed the expectations of their customers in a rapidly changing world.

Chapter 6
Providing Exceptional Customer Service

Exceptional customer service is the cornerstone of building strong, long-lasting relationships with your clients/customers. It's about going above and beyond to meet their needs, exceed their expectations, and leave a lasting impression. Here are some strategies to provide exceptional customer service:

Prioritize Responsiveness: In today's fast-paced world, customers expect prompt responses to their inquiries and concerns. Make it a priority to respond to customer queries promptly, whether through email, phone, or live chat. Aim to acknowledge their messages within hours, if not minutes, to demonstrate your comm tment to excellent service.

Empower Your Team: Equip your team with the knowledge, tools, and authority they need to address customer issues effectively. Provide comprehensive training on product knowledge, communication skills, and conflict resolution techniques. Empower frontline employees to make decisions and resolve issues on the spot, reducing the need for escalation and enhancing the customer experience.

Personalize Interactions: Treat each customer as an individual with unique needs and preferences. Personalize your interactions by using their name, referencing past interactions or purchases, and tailoring your recommendations to their specific situation. Show genuine interest in their concerns and goals, and demonstrate empathy and understanding in your communication.

Anticipate Customer Needs: Proactively anticipate and address customer needs before they arise. Use data analytics to identify patterns and trends in customer behavior, enabling you to predict their needs and preferences. Offer proactive support and guidance, such as proactive product recommendations, timely reminders, or educational resources, to enhance the customer experience and foster loyalty.

Provide Seamless Omnichannel Support: Customers expect a seamless experience across multiple channels, whether it's your website, social media, email, or phone. Ensure consistency in branding, messaging, and service quality across all touchpoints. Implement an omnichannel support strategy that allows customers to reach you through their preferred channels and seamlessly transition between channels w thout having to repeat themselves.

Solicit and Act on Feedback: Actively solicit feedback from your customers to identify areas for improvement and opportunities to enhance the customer experience. Use surveys, feedback forms, and customer satisfaction scores to gather insights into their satisfaction levels and pain points. Act on this feedback by implementing changes, addressing concerns, and continually striving to improve your products and services.

Exceed Expectations: Surprise and delight your customers by exceeding their expectations at every opportunity. Offer unexpected perks, bonuses, or discounts to show appreciation for their loyalty. Anticipate their needs and proactively offer solutions or assistance before they even ask. By consistently exceeding expectations, you can create memorable experiences that leave a lasting impression on your customers.

Providing exceptional customer service isn't just about resolving issues—it's about building trust, fostering loyalty, and creating advocates for your brand. By prioritizing responsiveness, personalization, proactive support, and continuous improvement, you can differentiate your business and build strong, long-lasting relationships with your clients/customers.

Chapter 7
Personalization and Customization

In today's hyper-connected world, customers crave experiences that are tailored to their individual preferences and needs. Personalization and customization are powerful tools for building deeper connections with your clients/customers, enhancing their satisfaction, and driving loyalty. Here's how you can leverage personalization and customization to nurture stronger client/customer relationships:

Collect and Utilize Customer Data: Start by collecting relevant customer data across various touchpoints, including interactions with your website, email engagement, purchase history, and demographic information. Utilize customer relationship management (CRM) systems or other data management tools to organize and analyze this data effectively. Use insights gleaned from customer data to personalize your interactions, recommend relevant products or services, and anticipate their needs.

Segment Your Audience: Divide your customer base into distinct segments based on shared characteristics, behaviors, or preferences. Common segmentation criteria include demographics (age, gender, location), psychographics (lifestyle, values, interests), purchase behavior (frequency, average order value), and engagement level (active vs. inactive customers). Tailor your marketing messages, product recommendations, and promotions to each segment's unique needs and preferences.

Dynamic Content and Recommendations: Leverage dynamic content and recommendation engines to deliver personalized experiences to your clients/customers. Dynamically adjust website content, product recommendations, and email campaigns based on each customer's behavior, preferences, and past interactions. Use machine learning algorithms to analyze historical data and predict future behavior, enabling you to deliver hyper-targeted content and recommendations.

Personalized Communication: Customize your communication with clients/customers to make it more relevant and engaging. Address them by name in your emails, newsletters, and marketing messages. Reference past interactions, purchases, or preferences to demonstrate that you understand their needs and value their business. Tailor your messaging and tone to resonate with each customer segment, whether it's formal and professional or casual and friendly.

Offer Customizable Products or Services: Give customers the ability to customize products or services to suit their individual preferences and tastes. Offer configurable options, such as color choices, sizing options, or feature selections, that allow customers to personalize their purchases. Provide interactive tools or configurators on your website that guide customers through the customization process and visualize the end result.

Personalized Loyalty Programs: Develop personalized loyalty programs that reward customers for their engagement, purchases, and advocacy. Offer personalized incentives, rewards, and perks based on each customer's unique preferences and behavior. Use data-driven insights to identify opportunities to incentivize desired behaviors and drive repeat purchases.

Listen and Respond to Feedback: Actively solicit feedback from customers about their preferences, experiences, and suggestions for improvement. Use this feedback to refine your personalization strategies, identify areas for enhancement, and address any pain points or concerns. Demonstrate that you value their input by acknowledging their feedback and taking action to incorporate their suggestions.

By prioritizing personalization and customization in your interactions with clients/customers, you can create memorable experiences that resonate on a personal level and foster deeper connections. Whether through targeted marketing campaigns, customized product offerings, or personalized communication, embracing personalization can set your business apart and drive long-term loyalty and advocacy.

Chapter 8
Managing Client/Customer Feedback and Reviews

Client/customer feedback and reviews are invaluable sources of insights that can help you understand your audience better, identify areas for improvement, and foster trust and credibility. Effectively managing feedback and reviews allows you to leverage them as powerful tools for enhancing the customer experience and driving business growth. Here's how you can effectively manage client/customer feedback and reviews:

Establish Feedback Channels: Provide multiple channels through which clients/customers can share their feedback and reviews, including email, website forms, social media, and online review platforms. Make it easy for them to provide feedback by offering simple and intuitive feedback mechanisms, such as rating scales, comment boxes, or surveys.

Monitor Feedback Proactively: Monitor client/customer feedback and reviews proactively to stay informed about what customers are saying about your products, services, and brand. Set up alerts and notifications to receive real-time updates whenever new feedback or reviews are posted online. Regularly check your feedback channels to ensure timely responses to customer inquiries and concerns.

Acknowledge and Respond Promptly: Acknowledge all client/customer feedback and reviews promptly, even if they are negative or critical. Respond to feedback in a timely and empathetic manner, expressing gratitude for their input and addressing any concerns or issues raised. Demonstrate that you value customer feedback and are committed to addressing their needs and improving their experience.

Encourage Positive Reviews: Encourage satisfied clients/customers to leave positive reviews and testimonials to share their positive experiences with others. Prompt them to leave reviews after completing a purchase, engaging with your services, or receiving exceptional customer service. Make it easy for them to leave reviews by providing direct links or instructions on how to do so.

Handle Negative Reviews Professionally: Handle negative reviews with professionalism and grace, refraining from becoming defensive or dismissive. Take the time to understand the customer's perspective and address their concerns constructively. Apologize for any shortcomings or issues they experienced, and offer solutions or remedies to rectify the situation. Use negative reviews as learning opportunities to identify areas for improvement and prevent similar issues in the future.

Aggregate and Analyze Feedback Data: Aggregate and analyze client/customer feedback data systematically to identify trends, patterns, and common themes. Use feedback analysis tools and techniques to categorize feedback by topic, sentiment, and urgency. Extract actionable insights from feedback data to inform strategic decision-making, product development, and customer experience enhancements.

Implement Changes and Improvements: Use client/customer feedback as a roadmap for implementing changes and improvements to your products, services, and processes. Prioritize feedback items based on their impact and feasibility, and develop action plans to address them systematically. Communicate with clients/customers about the changes you've made in response to their feedback, demonstrating your commitment to continuous improvement.

Celebrate Positive Feedback: Celebrate and showcase positive feedback and testimonials from satisfied clients/customers to reinforce trust and credibility in your brand. Share positive reviews on your website, social media channels, and marketing materials to build social proof and inspire confidence among prospective clients/customers.

By effectively managing client/customer feedback and reviews, you can harness the power of customer insights to drive business improvements, enhance the customer experience, and build stronger, more meaningful relationships with your audience. Embrace feedback as a valuable resource for growth and innovation, and demonstrate your commitment to listening, learning, and evolving based on customer input.

Chapter 9
Handling Complaints and Resolving Issues

In the realm of client/customer relationships, complaints and issues are inevitable. How you handle these challenges can make all the difference in retaining customer loyalty and enhancing your reputation. Here's how to effectively handle complaints and resolve issues:

Create a Clear Complaint Resolution Process: Establish a clear and transparent process for handling complaints and resolving issues within your organization. Outline the steps involved, from initial complaint receipt to final resolution, and communicate this process to your team members. Ensure that all employees are trained on the complaint resolution process and empowered to take appropriate action when faced with customer complaints.

Listen Actively and Empathetically: When a customer brings forth a complaint or issue, listen actively and empathetically to their concerns. Allow them to express their frustrations or dissatisfaction without interruption, and demonstrate genuine empathy for their situation. Acknowledge their feelings and assure them that their concerns are being taken seriously.

Apologize Sincerely: Offer a sincere apology to the customer for any inconvenience or dissatisfaction they have experienced. Regardless of who is at fault, taking responsibility for the situation and expressing regret can go a long way toward diffusing tension and rebuilding trust. Apologize without making excuses or shifting blame, and focus on finding a resolution to the problem at hand.

Investigate and Gather Information: Take the time to thoroughly investigate the customer's complaint or issue to understand the root cause and identify possible solutions. Gather all relevant information, including customer interactions, purchase history, and any other pertinent details. Consult with relevant team members or departments to gain additional insights and perspectives.

Offer a Solution or Compensation: Once you've identified the underlying issue, propose a solution or course of action to address the customer's concerns. Be proactive in offering a resolution that is fair, reasonable, and aligned with the customer's expectations. Depending on the severity of the issue, you may also consider offering compensation or restitution as a gesture of goodwill.

Follow Up and Ensure Satisfaction: After implementing a solution, follow up with the customer to ensure that they are satisfied with the outcome. Confirm that the issue has been resolved to their satisfaction and address any lingering concerns or questions they may have. Express gratitude for their patience and understanding throughout the resolution process.

Learn and Improve: Use complaints and issues as opportunities for learning and improvement within your organization. Analyze patterns and trends in customer complaints to identify underlying issues or areas for improvement in your products, services, or processes. Implement corrective actions and preventive measures to minimize the likelihood of similar issues occurring in the future.

Document and Share Insights: Document all customer complaints and resolutions in a central database or CRM system for future reference and analysis. Share insights and learnings from complaint resolution processes with relevant team members or departments to foster a culture of continuous improvement and customer-centricity.

By handling complaints and resolving issues effectively, you can turn negative experiences into opportunities to strengthen customer relationships, demonstrate your commitment to customer satisfaction, and enhance your reputation in the marketplace. Embrace complaints as valuable feedback for improvement, and prioritize swift and empathetic resolution to uphold customer trust and loyalty.

Part III: Leveraging Technology and Automation

Welcome to Part III of our journey towards optimizing client/customer relationships through the power of technology and automation. In this section, we delve into the transformative potential of leveraging cutting-edge tools and automation so utions to enhance efficiency, streamline operations, and drive meaningful connections with your clientele.

Choosing the Right Tools for Your Business

Selecting the right tools is paramount to the success of any business endeavor. In this segment, we explore the criteria and considerations for choosing the tools and technologies best suited to your unique needs and objectives. From CRM platforms to marketing automation software, we'll guide you through the process of identifying and implementing the tools that will propel your business forward.

Implementing Automation in Client/Customer Relationship Management

Automation has revolutionized the way businesses manage client/customer relationships. In this chapter, we dive into the strategies and best practices for implementing automation solutions to streamline CRM processes, enhance productivity, and deliver personalized experiences at scale. Discover how automation can empower your team to focus on high-value activities and nurture stronger connections with your clientele.

Data Management and Analysis for Improved Relationships

Data is the lifeblood of modern business, offering invaluable insights into customer behavior, preferences, and trends. In this section, we explore the importance of effective data management and analysis in cultivating deeper relationships with your clientele. Learn how to harness the power of data to tailor your offerings, anticipate needs, and drive personalized experiences that resonate with your audience.

Integrating Technology with Human Touch

While technology offers unparalleled efficiency and scalability, it's essential to balance automation with the human touch. In this chapter, we delve into the art of integrating technology with human empathy and intuition to create meaningful connections with your clients/customers. Discover how to leverage technology to enhance, rather than replace, human interactions and foster genuine relationships that drive loyalty and advocacy.

Join us as we embark on a journey to unlock the full potential of technology and automation in revolutionizing client/customer relationships. By mastering the art of choosing the right tools, implementing automation effectively, harnessing the power of data, and integrating technology with human touch, you'll be equipped to navigate the complexities of modern business and drive sustainable growth through meaningful connections with your clientele.

Chapter 10
Choosing the Right Tools for Your Business

Selecting the right software tools for your business is essential for maximizing efficiency, productivity, and effectiveness. With a plethora of options available in the market, it's crucial to identify tools that align with your business goals, requirements, and budget. Here are key considerations when choosing software tools for your business:

Scalability: Choose tools that can grow with your business. Look for scalable solutions that can accommodate increasing volumes of data, users, and transactions as your business expands.

Customization: Opt for software that offers customization options to tailor the solution to your unique business needs and workflows. Customizable features and configurations ensure that the software adapts to your specific requirements, rather than forcing you to conform to rigid processes.

Integration Capabilities: Prioritize software tools that seamlessly integrate with your existing systems, applications, and workflows. Integration capabilities allow for data sharing and synchronization across different platforms, eliminating silos and streamlining operations.

User-Friendly Interface: Choose intuitive and user-friendly software with a simple interface and navigation. An intuitive interface reduces the learning curve for users and enhances adoption rates, ensuring that your team can maximize the benefits of the software quickly and effectively.

Mobile Accessibility: In today's mobile-driven world, mobile accessibility is essential for flexibility and productivity. Look for software solutions that offer mobile apps or responsive web interfaces, allowing users to access key features and functionality on the go, anytime, anywhere.

Security and Compliance: Prioritize software tools that prioritize data security and compliance with industry regulations and standards. Look for features such as encryption, access controls, and compliance certifications to safeguard sensitive information and protect your business from security threats and legal risks.

Support and Training: Choose software vendors that offer comprehensive support, training, and resources to help you maximize the value of the software. Look for vendors that provide user guides, tutorials, training sessions, and responsive customer support to address any questions or issues that may arise.

Cost-Effectiveness: Consider the total cost of ownership, including upfront costs, subscription fees, implementation costs, and ongoing maintenance expenses. Choose software solutions that offer a favorable return on investment (ROI) by delivering tangible benefits and efficiencies that outweigh the costs.

By carefully evaluating these factors and selecting software tools that align with your business objectives and requirements, you can lay the foundation for success and unlock new opportunities for growth and innovation. In the following sections, we'll explore how to implement automation in client/customer relationship management, manage data effectively, and integrate technology seamlessly with the human touch to enhance client/customer experiences.

Chapter 11
Implementing Automation in Client/Customer Relationship Management

In today's fast-paced business environment, managing client/customer relationships efficiently is crucial for sustainable growth. Automation can play a pivotal role in streamlining client/customer relationship management (CRM) processes, improving productivity, and enhancing the overall customer experience. Here's how you can implement automation in CRM effectively:

Lead Management Automation: Automate lead capture, qualification, and nurturing processes to streamline your sales pipeline. Use automated lead scoring algorithms to prioritize leads based on their likelihood to convert, allowing your sales team to focus their efforts on high-potential prospects. Implement automated email workflows to nurture leads through the sales funnel, delivering relevant content and communications at each stage of the buyer's journey.

Contact Management Automation: Simplify contact management tasks by automating data entry, updates, and segmentation. Integrate your CRM system with other tools and databases to automatically sync contact information and ensure data accuracy. Use automation rules to categorize contacts based on criteria such as industry, location, or engagement level, allowing for targeted communication and personalized outreach.

Task and Reminder Automation: Automate task assignment, scheduling, and reminders to ensure timely follow-up and engagement with clients/customers. Set up automated alerts and notifications to remind your team members of upcoming deadlines, meetings, or follow-up actions. Use task automation to assign tasks based on predefined triggers, such as new leads or customer inquiries, streamlining workflow management and enhancing productivity.

Email Marketing Automation: Leverage email marketing automation to deliver personalized and timely communications to your clients/customers. Use automated email campaigns to send welcome emails, promotional offers, newsletters, and follow-up messages based on customer behavior and preferences. Segment your email list based on demographics, purchase history, or engagement level to tailor content and offers to specific audience segments.

Customer Support Automation: Enhance the efficiency of your customer support operations by implementing automation for ticket routing, response prioritization, and resolution workflows. Use chatbots and virtual assistants to handle routine inquiries and FAQs, freeing up human agents to focus on more complex issues and personalized interactions. Implement self-service portals and knowledge bases to empower customers to find answers to their questions independently.

Feedback and Survey Automation: Automate the collection and analysis of client/customer feedback and survey responses to gain valuable insights into satisfaction levels, preferences, and areas for improvement. Use automated survey tools to send out customer satisfaction surveys, product feedback forms, or Net Promoter Score (NPS) surveys at strategic touchpoints throughout the customer journey. Analyze survey data in real-time to identify trends, patterns, and actionable insights for enhancing the customer experience.

Analytics and Reporting Automation: Streamline the process of data analysis and reporting by automating the generation of custom reports, dashboards, and performance metrics. Use CRM analytics tools to track key performance indicators (KPIs), monitor sales performance, and measure customer satisfaction levels. Automate the scheduling and distribution of reports to relevant stakeholders, ensuring timely access to actionable insights for informed decision-making.

By implementing automation in client/customer relationship management, you can streamline processes, improve efficiency, and deliver more personalized and seamless experiences to your clients/customers. Automation enables you to focus your resources on high-value activities, drive productivity gains, and ultimately, build stronger and more profitable relationships with your clientele.

Chapter 12
Data Management and Analysis for Improved Relationships

In the digital age, data has become a valuable asset for small businesses seeking to understand their clients/customers better, anticipate their needs, and tailor experiences to drive engagement and loyalty. Effective data management and analysis are essential for extracting actionable insights from the wealth of information available and leveraging it to nurture stronger and more meaningful relationships with your clientele. Here's how you can harness the power of data management and analysis to improve client/customer relationships:

Centralized Data Repository: Establish a centralized data repository to store and manage all client/customer-related information in a structured and organized manner. Use customer relationship management (CRM) systems or database solutions to consolidate data from various sources, including sales transactions, interactions, communications, and feedback. A centralized repository ensures data consistency, accessibility, and security, enabling you to gain a holistic view of your clients/customers' profiles and interactions.

Data Quality Assurance: Ensure data accuracy, completeness, and integrity by implementing data quality assurance processes and protocols. Regularly clean and validate data to identify and correct errors, duplicates, and inconsistencies. Enforce data governance policies and standards to maintain data quality standards and compliance with regulatory requirements. Clean and accurate data form the foundation for reliable analysis and decision-making, enhancing the effectiveness of your client/customer relationship management efforts.

Segmentation and Personalization: Utilize data segmentation techniques to categorize clients/customers into distinct groups based on shared characteristics, behaviors, or preferences. Segment data by demographic attributes, purchase history, engagement level, or psychographic traits to create targeted audience segments for personalized marketing and communication strategies. Leverage data-driven personalization to deliver relevant content, offers, and experiences that resonate with each segment's unique needs and preferences, fostering deeper connections and engagement.

Predictive Analytics: Harness the power of predictive analytics to anticipate client/customer behavior, preferences, and future needs. Use predictive modeling techniques, such as machine learning algorithms, to analyze historical data patterns and identify trends, correlations, and predictive indicators. Predictive analytics enable you to forecast customer lifetime value, churn propensity, purchase likelihood, and other key metrics, empowering you to proactively tailor your strategies and interventions to maximize customer satisfaction and retention.

Customer Journey Mapping: Map out the client/customer journey across various touchpoints and interactions to gain insights into their experiences, pain points, and opportunities for improvement. Use data analytics tools and techniques to track and analyze customer interactions at each stage of the journey, from initial awareness to post-purchase support. Identify friction points, bottlenecks, and areas of delight to optimize the customer experience and drive loyalty and advocacy.

Sentiment Analysis: Leverage sentiment analysis tools to analyze client/customer feedback, reviews, and social media interactions to gauge sentiment, attitudes, and emotions. Use natural language processing (NLP) algorithms to extract insights from unstructured text data, such as customer reviews, comments, and social media posts. Sentiment analysis enables you to identify positive sentiment, negative sentiment, and emerging trends, allowing you to respond promptly to customer feedback, mitigate issues, and capitalize on opportunities to enhance satisfaction and loyalty.

Continuous Improvement: Embrace a culture of continuous improvement by using data insights to inform strategic decision-making and optimize client/customer relationship management practices. Regularly analyze performance metrics, KPIs, and customer feedback to identify areas for enhancement and innovation. Experiment with new strategies, tactics, and technologies to test hypotheses, iterate on approaches, and drive incremental improvements in client/customer relationships and business outcomes.

By prioritizing data management and analysis for improved client/customer relationships, small businesses can unlock valuable insights, drive personalized experiences, and foster deeper connections with their clientele. Data-driven decision-making enables businesses to anticipate needs, mitigate risks, and capitalize on opportunities, ultimately driving growth, loyalty, and competitive advantage in an increasingly digital and data-driven marketplace.

Chapter 13
Integrating Technology with Human Touch

In the era of digital transformation, it's easy to get caught up in the allure of technology and automation. While these tools undoubtedly offer numerous benefits for streamlining processes and enhancing efficiency, they must be balanced with the human touch—the personal, empathetic, and human elements that form the foundation of meaningful client/customer relationships. Here's how you can integrate technology with human touch to create exceptional experiences and foster deeper connections with your clientele:

Personalized Communication: While automated communication tools such as email marketing platforms and chatbots can facilitate efficient communication at scale, they should be complemented by personalized, humanized interactions. Incorporate personal touches into your communications, such as addressing clients/customers by name, referencing past interactions or preferences, and expressing genuine interest and empathy in their needs and concerns. By adding a human touch to your communications, you can create a sense of connection and rapport that resonates with your audience on a deeper level.

Empathetic Customer Support: While self-service portals and automated support channels can provide quick resolutions to routine inquiries and issues, there are times when clients/customers need the reassurance and empathy that only a human agent can provide. Invest in well-trained customer support representatives who possess strong interpersonal skills, empathy, and problem-solving abilities. Empower your team to go above and beyond to listen to clients/customers' concerns, understand their perspectives, and provide personalized solutions that address their unique needs and circumstances.

Strategic Touchpoints: Use technology to identify strategic touchpoints throughout the client/customer journey where human intervention can make a meaningful impact. Whether it's a personalized follow-up call after a significant purchase, a handwritten thank-you note for a long-standing client, or a face-to-face meeting to discuss complex needs or challenges, strategically integrate human touchpoints into your customer experience strategy. These moments of personal connection demonstrate your commitment to building authentic relationships and exceeding expectations.

Tailored Recommendations: Leverage technology-driven data analysis and recommendation engines to provide clients/customers with personalized recommendations and solutions tailored to their preferences and interests. Use algorithms to analyze past behavior, purchase history, and engagement patterns to predict future needs and preferences. Then, complement these data-driven recommendations with human expertise and intuition to offer additional insights, context, and personalized advice that resonates with your clientele.

Cultivate Emotional Connections: While technology can facilitate transactions and automate processes, it's the emotional connections forged through genuine human interactions that truly differentiate a brand. Focus on cultivating emotional connections with your clients/customers by demonstrating empathy, authenticity, and vulnerability. Show appreciation for their loyalty and support, celebrate milestones and achievements together, and acknowledge their contributions to your success. By fostering emotional connections, you can create loyal advocates who are deeply invested in your brand and mission.

Feedback and Collaboration: Use technology to facilitate ongoing feedback and collaboration with your clients/customers, but don't underestimate the power of face-to-face interactions and open dialogue. Schedule regular check-ins, meetings, or events where you can engage directly with clients/customers to solicit feedback, share updates, and collaborate on solutions. These opportunities for real-time interaction allow for deeper understanding, mutual trust, and co-creation of value, strengthening the partnership between your business and its clientele.

Human-Centric Culture: Finally, foster a human-centric culture within your organization that prioritizes empathy, authenticity, and connection in every interaction with clients/customers. Lead by example and empower your team to embrace the human side of business, encouraging them to listen actively, communicate authentically, and go the extra mile to exceed expectations. By embodying human values and principles in your business practices, you can create a culture of trust, collaboration, and mutual respect that resonates with clients/customers and sets your brand apart in a crowded marketplace.

By integrating technology with human touch, small businesses can achieve the perfect balance between efficiency and empathy, automation and authenticity. By leveraging technology to enhance, rather than replace, human connections, you can create exceptional experiences that foster loyalty, trust, and long-lasting relationships with your clientele. Ultimately, it's the combination of technological innovation and human empathy that drives meaningful engagement and drives business success in the digital age.

Part IV: Scaling Through Client/Customer Relationships

In this final section, we'll explore strategies for leveraging client/customer relationships to scale your business and drive sustainable growth. By focusing on referral programs, word-of-mouth marketing, social media, digital marketing, long-term loyalty, repeat business, and measuring success, you can cultivate a loyal customer base, expand your reach, and adapt your strategies for continued success.

Leveraging Referral Programs and Word-of-Mouth Marketing

Referral programs and word-of-mouth marketing are powerful tools for acquiring new clients/customers and expanding your business's reach. Encourage satisfied clients/customers to refer their friends, family, and colleagues by offering incentives such as discounts, rewards, or exclusive perks for successful referrals. Leverage word-of-mouth marketing by providing exceptional experiences that inspire clients/customers to share their positive experiences with others, both online and offline.

Expanding Your Reach Through Social Media and Digital Marketing

Harness the power of social media and digital marketing to amplify your brand's reach and visibility. Establish a strong presence on social media platforms where your target audience congregates, and engage with them through compelling content, interactive experiences, and personalized communication. Leverage digital marketing channels such as email marketing, content marketing, search engine optimization (SEO), and paid advertising to attract, engage, and convert prospects into loyal clients/customers.

Building Long-Term Loyalty and Repeat Business

Focus on building long-term loyalty and fostering repeat business by delivering exceptional experiences and personalized service. Invest in relationship-building initiatives such as loyalty programs, VIP perks, and exclusive offers to reward and incentivize repeat purchases. Continuously exceed expectations, anticipate needs, and demonstrate your commitment to client/customer satisfaction to cultivate lasting loyalty and advocacy.

Measuring Success and Adapting Strategies

Measure the success of your client/customer relationship initiatives by tracking key performance indicators (KPIs) such as customer acquisition cost (CAC), customer lifetime value (CLV), retention rate, referral rate, and Net Promoter Score (NPS). Analyze data and feedback to assess the effectiveness of your strategies and identify areas for improvement. Adapt your strategies based on insights gleaned from data analysis and client/customer feedback to optimize performance and drive continuous improvement.

By leveraging referral programs, word-of-mouth marketing, social media, digital marketing, long-term loyalty, repeat business, and measuring success, you can scale your business through client/customer relationships effectively. By prioritizing the cultivation of loyal, engaged clients/customers and continuously refining your strategies based on data-driven insights, you can achieve sustainable growth and success in today's competitive marketplace.

Chapter 14
Leveraging Referral Programs and Word-of-Mouth Marketing

Referral programs and word-of-mouth marketing are invaluable assets for small businesses looking to expand their client/customer base and drive growth. Leveraging the power of satisfied clients/customers who refer their friends, family, and colleagues can lead to higher conversion rates, lower acquisition costs, and increased brand credibility. In this chapter, we'll explore strategies for designing and implementing effective referral programs and maximizing the impact of word-of-mouth marketing.

Designing a Referral Program:

Clear Incentives: Offer compelling incentives for clients/customers to refer others to your business. This could include discounts, exclusive offers, loyalty points, or even cash rewards. Ensure that the incentives are attractive enough to motivate action but still aligned with your business goals and profitability.

Simple Process: Keep the referral process simple and straightforward to encourage participation. Provide clients/customers with easy-to-use referral tools, such as referral links or personalized codes, and clearly outline the steps they need to take to refer others. Minimize friction points and make it as easy as possible for clients/customers to refer their contacts.

Transparency and Trust: Build trust and transparency into your referral program by clearly communicating the terms and conditions, eligibility criteria, and reward structure. Ensure that clients/customers understand how the program works and what they can expect in return for their referrals. Avoid any hidden fees or complicated rules that could deter participation or erode trust.

Promotion and Awareness: Promote your referral program through various channels to maximize visibility and reach. Use email marketing, social media, website banners, and in-store signage to inform clients/customers about the program and encourage participation. Highlight the benefits of referring others and showcase success stories to demonstrate the value of participation.

Maximizing Word-of-Mouth Marketing:

Deliver Exceptional Experiences: The foundation of effective word-of-mouth marketing lies in delivering exceptional experiences that inspire clients/customers to share their positive experiences with others. Focus on exceeding expectations, providing personalized service, and resolving issues promptly to create advocates for your brand who will enthusiastically recommend your business to others.

Encourage Reviews and Testimonials: Actively encourage clients/customers to leave reviews and testimonials on platforms such as Google, Yelp, and social media. Positive reviews and testimonials serve as social proof of your business's credibility and can influence purchasing decisions for prospective clients/customers. Provide incentives or rewards for leaving reviews to incentivize participation.

Facilitate Referral Opportunities: Create opportunities for clients/customers to naturally refer others to your business through their networks. This could involve hosting referral events, offering referral-only promotions or discounts, or providing referral cards that clients/customers can share with their contacts. Empower clients/customers to become brand ambassadors and advocates for your business.

Nurture Relationships: Cultivate strong relationships with clients/customers by staying engaged, providing value, and demonstrating appreciation for their loyalty and support. Regularly communicate with clients/customers through newsletters, personalized messages, and follow-up interactions to stay top-of-mind and reinforce positive associations with your brand.

By leveraging referral programs and word-of-mouth marketing, small businesses can tap into the power of satisfied clients/customers to drive organic growth and expand their client/customer base. By designing a compelling referral program, delivering exceptional experiences, and nurturing relationships with clients/customers, businesses can harness the influence of word-of-mouth marketing to amplify their reach and credibility in the marketplace.

Chapter 15: Expanding Your Reach Through Social Media and Digital Marketing

In today's interconnected world, social media and digital marketing offer powerful channels for expanding your business's reach, engaging with your target audience, and driving growth. By leveraging these platforms effectively, you can connect with potential clients/customers, build brand awareness, and drive traffic to your products or services. Here's how you can harness the power of social media and digital marketing to expand your reach:

Identify Your Target Audience: Before diving into social media and digital marketing efforts, it's essential to understand your target audience's demographics, interests, and behaviors. Conduct market research to identify where your audience spends time online, what platforms they use, and what type of content resonates with them. This understanding will guide your strategy and help you effectively reach and engage your audience.

Establish a Strong Social Media Presence: Choose the social media platforms that align with your target audience and business objectives. Whether it's Facebook, Instagram, Twitter, LinkedIn, or others, create compelling profiles that reflect your brand's identity and values. Consistently post relevant and engaging content that provides value to your audience, such as informative articles, entertaining videos, or behind-the-scenes glimpses into your business.

Engage with Your Audience: Social media is not just a broadcasting platform—it's a two-way communication channel. Engage with your audience by responding to comments, messages, and mentions promptly. Encourage conversations, ask questions, and solicit feedback to foster a sense of community and connection with your followers. By actively engaging with your audience, you can build trust, loyalty, and brand advocacy over time.

Utilize Paid Advertising: Social media platforms offer robust advertising options that allow you to target specific demographics, interests, and behaviors with precision. Invest in paid advertising campaigns to expand your reach and amplify your message to a broader audience. Experiment with different ad formats, targeting options, and messaging strategies to optimize your campaigns for maximum effectiveness and return on investment.

Create Compelling Content: Content is king in the digital marketing landscape. Create high-quality, compelling content that resonates with your target audience and adds value to their lives. Whether it's blog posts, videos, infographics, or podcasts, focus on producing content that educates, entertains, or inspires your audience. Tailor your content to each social media platform's format and audience preferences to maximize engagement and visibility.

Leverage Influencer Marketing: Partner with influencers in your industry or niche to extend your reach and credibility. Identify influencers whose values and audience align with your brand, and collaborate with them on sponsored content, product reviews, or brand endorsements. Influencers can help amplify your message and introduce your brand to their followers, driving awareness and consideration among new audiences.

Monitor and Measure Performance: Track key performance indicators (KPIs) such as reach, engagement, website traffic, and conversion rates to gauge the effectiveness of your social media and digital marketing efforts. Use analytics tools provided by social media platforms and digital marketing channels to monitor performance, identify trends, and make data-driven decisions to optimize your strategy over time.

By leveraging social media and digital marketing channels effectively, you can expand your reach, engage with your audience, and drive growth for your business. By understanding your target audience, establishing a strong social media presence, engaging with your audience, utilizing paid advertising, creating compelling content, leveraging influencer marketing, and monitoring performance, you can maximize the impact of your efforts and achieve your business objectives in the digital landscape.

Chapter 16
Building Long-Term Loyalty and Repeat Business

Building long-term loyalty and fostering repeat business is essential for the sustained success of any business. Loyal customers not only provide a steady revenue stream but also act as brand advocates, driving new customer acquisition through word-of-mouth referrals. Here's how you can cultivate long-term loyalty and encourage repeat business:

Deliver Consistent Value: Consistency is key to building trust and loyalty with your customers. Consistently deliver high-quality products or services that meet or exceed customer expectations. Provide exceptional customer service at every touchpoint, from pre-purchase inquiries to post-sale support. By consistently delivering value, you can earn your customers' trust and loyalty over time.

Personalize the Customer Experience: Tailor your interactions and communications to each customer's preferences and needs. Use data analytics to segment your customer base and personalize your marketing messages, product recommendations, and promotions. Address customers by name, acknowledge their past purchases, and anticipate their future needs to create a personalized experience that resonates with them on an individual level.

Reward Loyalty: Implement a loyalty program to reward customers for their repeat business and ongoing support. Offer incentives such as discounts, rewards points, exclusive offers, or VIP perks for loyal customers. Show appreciation for their loyalty by acknowledging milestones, such as anniversaries or milestones in their customer journey, and rewarding them for their continued patronage.

Stay Connected: Stay connected with your customers beyond the point of sale. Engage with them regularly through email newsletters, social media, or other communication channels to keep your brand top-of-mind. Provide valuable content, tips, and resources that add value to their lives and reinforce your brand's expertise and authority in your industry.

Seek Feedback and Act on It: Actively solicit feedback from your customers to understand their needs, preferences, and pain points. Use surveys, feedback forms, or customer reviews to gather insights into their experiences with your products or services. Listen attentively to their feedback and take action to address any issues or concerns promptly. By demonstrating that you value their input and are committed to continuously improving, you can strengthen trust and loyalty with your customers.

Encourage Referrals and Advocacy: Encourage satisfied customers to refer their friends, family, and colleagues to your business. Offer incentives or rewards for successful referrals to incentivize word-of-mouth marketing. Cultivate brand advocates by providing exceptional experiences and value, and empower them to share their positive experiences with others. Referral marketing is one of the most effective ways to drive new customer acquisition and foster long-term loyalty.

Stay Competitive: Keep an eye on your competitors and industry trends to ensure that you remain competitive in the marketplace. Continuously innovate and evolve your products, services, and customer experiences to stay ahead of the curve and meet changing customer expectations. By staying relevant and offering value that sets you apart from competitors, you can retain loyal customers and encourage repeat business.

By prioritizing long-term loyalty and repeat business, you can create a sustainable foundation for growth and success. By consistently delivering value, personalizing the customer experience, rewarding loyalty, staying connected, seeking feedback, encouraging referrals, and staying competitive, you can cultivate strong, lasting relationships with your customers that drive repeat business and advocacy for your brand.

Chapter 16
Measuring Success and Adapting Strategies

In the dynamic landscape of business, measuring success and adapting strategies are essential components of sustainable growth. By establishing clear metrics, tracking key performance indicators (KPIs), and regularly evaluating the effectiveness of your strategies, you can identify areas of improvement, capitalize on opportunities, and stay ahead of the competition. Here's how you can effectively measure success and adapt your strategies for continued growth:

Define Clear Objectives and KPIs: Begin by clearly defining your business objectives and identifying key performance indicators (KPIs) that align with those objectives. Whether it's increasing sales revenue, improving customer satisfaction, or expanding market share, establish measurable goals and metrics to track your progress and evaluate success.

Implement Analytics and Reporting Tools: Utilize analytics and reporting tools to gather data and insights into your business performance. Invest in robust analytics platforms, customer relationship management (CRM) systems, and business intelligence tools that provide real-time visibility into key metrics and performance indicators. Use these tools to monitor progress, identify trends, and uncover opportunities for improvement.

Track and Analyze Performance Metrics: Regularly track and analyze performance metrics across all areas of your business, including sales, marketing, customer service, and operations. Monitor KPIs such as sales revenue, customer acquisition cost (CAC), customer lifetime value (CLV), retention rate, conversion rate, and customer satisfaction scores. Analyze trends, patterns, and correlations in your data to gain insights into what's working well and where adjustments are needed.

Gather Customer Feedback and Insights: Solicit feedback from your customers through surveys, feedback forms, and customer reviews to gain insights into their experiences and satisfaction levels. Pay attention to both quantitative metrics, such as Net Promoter Score (NPS) and Customer Satisfaction Score (CSAT), as well as qualitative feedback that provides deeper insights into customer needs, preferences, and pain points. Use customer feedback to identify areas for improvement and inform strategic decision-making.

Benchmark Against Competitors and Industry Standards: Benchmark your performance against competitors and industry standards to gain perspective on your relative performance and identify opportunities for differentiation. Analyze industry trends, competitive landscape, and best practices to identify areas where you can outperform competitors and gain a competitive advantage.

Experiment and Iterate: Embrace a culture of experimentation and iteration by testing new strategies, tactics, and initiatives. Implement A/B testing, pilot programs, and controlled experiments to evaluate the effectiveness of different approaches and identify what resonates best with your audience. Be willing to pivot and adapt your strategies based on data-driven insights and feedback from customers and stakeholders.

Stay Agile and Flexible: In today's rapidly changing business environment, agility and flexibility are critical for success. Stay nimble and responsive to market shifts, emerging trends, and changing customer preferences. Continuously monitor external factors such as economic conditions, technological advancements, and regulatory changes that may impact your business, and be prepared to adjust your strategies accordingly.

Regularly Review and Refine Strategies: Schedule regular strategy review sessions to assess the effectiveness of your current strategies and make adjustments as needed. Use data-driven insights, feedback from stakeholders, and lessons learned from past experiences to inform strategic decision-making. Be proactive in identifying opportunities for optimization and refinement to ensure that your business remains agile, competitive, and poised for growth.

By measuring success, gathering insights, and adapting strategies accordingly, you can position your business for sustained growth and success in today's dynamic marketplace. By establishing clear objectives and KPIs, implementing analytics tools, tracking performance metrics, gathering customer feedback, benchmarking against competitors, experimenting and iterating, staying agile and flexible, and regularly reviewing and refining strategies, you can navigate challenges, capitalize on opportunities, and drive continuous improvement and innovation within your organization.

Conclusion

As we come to the end of this journey exploring the significance of client/customer relationships in business, we reflect on the transformative power these connections hold and look forward to the continued growth and success of your entrepreneurial endeavors.

The Power of Client/Customer Relationships in Business Growth

Throughout this book, we've underscored the critical role that client/customer relationships play in driving business growth and success. From building trust and credibility to fostering loyalty and advocacy, these relationships serve as the cornerstone of sustainable business development. By prioritizing the cultivation of meaningful connections with your clientele, you unlock the key to unlocking untapped potential, driving revenue, and achieving long-term success.

As you implement the strategies and techniques outlined in this book, remember the immense impact that each client/customer interaction can have on your business's trajectory. By delivering exceptional experiences, providing personalized service, and leveraging technology and automation to enhance efficiency, you'll be well-positioned to nurture strong, lasting relationships with your clientele and drive continued growth and prosperity.

Looking Ahead: Continuing Your Entrepreneurial Journey

As you continue your entrepreneurial journey, remember that the pursuit of excellence is a never-ending endeavor. Embrace a mindset of continuous learning, adaptation, and innovation as you navigate the ever-evolving landscape of business. Stay agile, remain resilient, and be open to new opportunities and challenges that arise along the way.

Whether you're just starting out on your entrepreneurial path or are already well on your way, the journey ahead is bound to be filled with twists and turns, ups and downs. But by staying true to your vision, staying connected with your clientele, and staying committed to delivering value and excellence in everything you do, you'll be well-equipped to overcome obstacles, seize opportunities, and achieve your goals.

Thank you for joining us on this journey into the heart of client/customer relationships in business. May the insights and strategies shared in this book serve as valuable resources and inspiration as you chart your course towards success in the dynamic and ever-changing world of entrepreneurship. Here's to your continued growth, prosperity, and fulfillment in all your entrepreneurial endeavors.

www.ingramcontent.com/pod-product-compliance
Lightning Source LLC
Chambersburg PA
CBHW072329270726
48658CB00016B/2177